TURKEY

MAJOR WORLD NATIONS

TURKEY

Garry Lyle

CHELSEA HOUSE PUBLISHERS
Philadelphia

Chelsea House Publishers

Copyright © 2000 by Chelsea House Publishers,
a division of Main Line Book Co.
All rights reserved.
Printed in Malaysia

First Printing.

1 3 5 7 9 8 6 4 2

Library of Congress Cataloging-in-Publication Data

Lyle, Garry.
[Let's visit Turkey]
Turkey / Garry Lyle
p. cm. — (Major world nations)
Includes index.
Summary: An overview of the history geography, economy, government,
people, and culture of Turkey.
ISBN 0-7910-5401-2 (hc)
1. Turkey—Description and travel—Juvenile literature.
[1. Turkey.] I. Title. II. Series.
DR429.4.L95   1999
956.103—dc21   99-11867
CIP

ACKNOWLEDGEMENTS

The Author and Publishers are grateful to the following organizations and individuals
for permission to reproduce photographs in this book:
The Reverend J. C. Allen; Art Directors Photo Library; Michael Howarth; Spectrum
Colour Library; David Taylor; The Turkish Embassy; The Turkish Tourism Information
Office.

CONTENTS

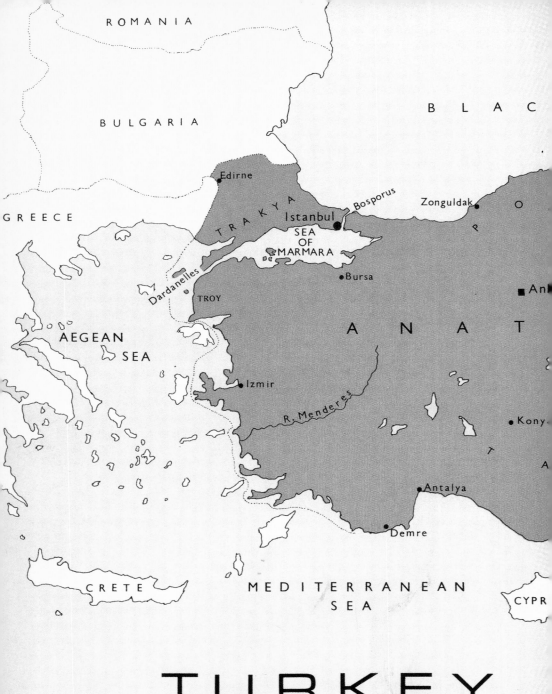

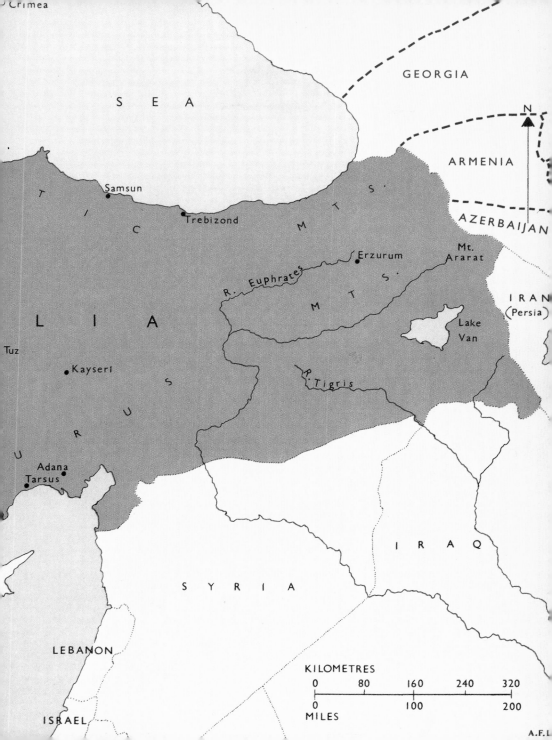

FACTS AT A GLANCE

Land and People

Official Name	Republic of Turkey
Location	Southwestern Asia bordering the Black Sea between Bulgaria and Georgia, and bordering the Aegean and Mediterranean seas between Greece and Syria.
Area	487, 862 square miles (780,580 square kilometers)
Climate	Western and southern Turkey have a Mediterranean climate / northern Turkey has a temperate climate
Capital	Ankara
Other Cities	Istanbul, Antalya, Izmir
Population	64,566,500
Major Rivers	Bosporus, Tigris, Euphrates,
Major Lakes	Sea of Marmara, Van, Tuz, Iznik
Mountains	Pontic, Taurus, Istranca
Highest Point	Mount Ararat, 3,228 feet (5,166 meters)

Official Language	Turkish
Other Languages	Kurdish, Arabic
Ethnic Groups	Turkish (80 percent), Kurdish (20 percent)
Religions	Muslim (99 percent)
Literacy Rate	82.3 percent
Average Life Expectancy	70.38 years (male); 75.39 years (female)

Economy

Natural Resources	Coal, chromium, iron ore, sulphur, copper, mercury
Division of Labor Force	Agriculture, 43.1 percent; service, 30.1 percent; industry, 14.4 percent
Agricultural Products	Hazelnuts, tea, tobacco, sugar beets, dates, livestock
Industries	Textiles and clothing, mining, petroleum
Major Imports	Machinery, fuels, raw materials
Major Exports	Textiles, clothing, carpets, iron and steel products, hazelnuts
Currency	Turkish lira

Government

Form of Government	Parliamentary republic
Government Bodies	National Assembly (parliament), Council of Ministers
Formal Head of State	President
Head of Government	Prime Minister
Voting Rights	All persons 18 years of age and older

HISTORY AT A GLANCE

9000 B.C.   First agrarian settlements in the world are established in what is now southern Turkey and northern Iraq.

2200-1200 B.C.   Hittites and Assyrians begin to settle into the land around Anatolia.

1200 B.C.   Greeks begin their takeover of the region and settle more of the land in Asia Minor.

559-529 B.C.   The Persians invade Asia Minor and take over much of the land held by the Greeks. They remain the rulers of Anatolia for more than two centuries.

334 B.C.   Alexander the Great of Macedonia, together with the Greeks, crosses the Hellespont River and drives the Persians out of Anatolia. Anatolia becomes a Greek country.

133 B.C.-305 A.D.   Rome takes over protection of Anatolia as a boundary of their expanding empire. The first Christian missionaries come to the area, among them Saint Paul, who is himself Anatolian.

330 A.D.   Christianity becomes the official religion of the whole Roman Empire. Emperor Constantine

10

establishes a new capital in Byzantium (later called Contantinople, and still later Istanbul).

1037 The Seljuk Turks, led by Alp Arslan, become rulers of Anatolia. Anatolia prospers under their control.

1300 Othman I (Osman) takes over control of Anatolia and becomes the sultan of Turkey. He begins building what would become the great Turkish Ottoman Empire.

1453 Constantinople falls to the Turks and becomes the capital city of the Ottoman Empire.

1609 Work begins on the famous Blue Mosque in Constantinople.

1683 This year marks the beginning of the decline of the Ottoman Empire's power after they fail to capture Vienna. Over the next century and a half, they gradually lose their holdings throughout Europe and most of Asia.

1853-1856 The Crimean War is fought, with Britain and France helping Turkey fight off the advances of the Russian army.

1914-1918 Turkey goes into World War I on the side of Germany which precipitates the final collapse of the Ottoman Empire.

1919-1922 Greek forces try to take over part of Turkey and are finally defeated by troops led by General Mustafa Kemal.

1923 On October 29, Turkey is proclaimed an independent republic with Ankara as its capital and Mustafa Kemal as its first president.

1923-1934	Under Kemal's leadership, sweeping reforms are introduced including formation of a parliament, introduction of the Latin alphabet and calendar, lifting of the requirement of veils for women, and introduction of surnanes. Kemal is given the surname Atatürk, meaning "Father of the Turks."
1930	Constantinople's name is officially changed to Istanbul.
1939-1945	Turkey is neutral through most of World War II, only declaring war on Germany in the final months of the war.
1950-1983	The transition to a multiparty democratic government is a difficult one and there are three military coups that occur at various times during the tansition.
1974	Turkey invades Cyprus to assist the Turkish people living there when Greece tries to annex the island. The island of Cyprus ends up divided and tensions between Turkey and Greece remain high.
1980	A military coup takes over the government.
1983	Elections are held for the first time since a military coup in 1980. The Kurdish Workers Party (PKK) begins a campaign of terror against Turkey to win independence as a Kurdish nation.
1987	Turkey applies for full membership in the European Union but is refused partly because of objections from Greece.
1993	Turkey's first female prime minister is appointed, Tnasu Çiller. The Kurdish conflict in the south continues with Turkish forces trying to put down

the Kurdish rebels. In March a truce is declared but in May the PKK (Kurds) ambush unarmed soldiers and civilians. The government begins to carry out air strikes against Kurdish bases in Iraq in December.

1996   The Kurdish problem continues with Turkish forces destroying Kurdish towns and persecuting Kurdish political leaders and scholars. The world community views these acts as human rights violations.

1997   Annual inflation reaches 99 percent and the bloody Kurdish struggle for independence continues in the southeastern part of Turkey. Turkey's problems with Greece and the Kurds continue to haunt the country when it is again refused admission to the European Union.

Mount Uludağ, a Turkish ski resort.

1

Country on Two Continents

If you would like to visit a country where you can begin the morning with snow sports and end it with some warm sea-bathing, you should try Turkey. Of course you would have to choose the right place, and the right time of the year. Turkey is a big country—bigger than any in western Europe—and much of its 4,500 miles (7,200 kilometers) of coastline is too cold for swimming when the snow on the mountains above is good for skiing. But you could certainly swim and ski on the same morning if you were to choose the south coast of Anatolia, where the Taurus Mountains slope down through groves of oranges and bananas to the warmest beaches of the Mediterranean Sea.

Anatolia is the main part of Turkey, and the most westerly part of Asia, the part which juts out towards southeastern Europe, and is sometimes called Asia Minor. It is also called Turkey in Asia, because Turkey is a country divided between

15

two continents. The other continent is Europe, where about 9,300 square miles (24,000 square kilometers) of Turkish territory face Anatolia across the small and nearly landlocked Sea of Marmara.

By contrast with Turkey in Asia, Turkey in Europe seems very small. Its land area is less than one thirtieth of the 301,000 square miles (780,000 square kilometers) covered by the whole country, and it has only a small percentage of the 70 million Turkish people. However, it is much more important to Turkey than its size might suggest. Not only does it give the Turks a place among the European nations and control of a "gateway" into Europe. It also contains their country's biggest and most famous city and seaport, Istanbul.

Under its older names of Byzantium and Constantinople, Istanbul was for many centuries the huge and beautiful center

A view of Istanbul, the city which forms the gateway between Turkey in Asia and Turkey in Europe.

of the Roman Empire. Later, it became the capital of a powerful Turkish empire which spread through north Africa, southeast Europe and much of western Asia. And although the Turks chose a new capital (Ankara in Anatolia) when their empire broke up, Istanbul is still a great and growing city. It is growing mainly because of its many factory industries, some of which were started with help from the United States and other friendly countries.

Old Istanbul and some of its modern suburbs lie along the western shore of the Bosporus, a strait linking the Sea of Marmara with the much bigger Black Sea. These shores were once the home of a Greek-speaking people, and Bosporus is a Greek name. It means "ox-crossing," and so can be likened to the English place-name Oxford. But Oxford was given its name because it was a place where farm cattle could cross the Thames River safely, while the name Bosporus came from an old Greek story about a girl named Io.

In the story, the god Zeus turned Io into a cow, to hide her from the jealous goddess Hera. Unluckily for Io, Hera saw through the disguise, and sent a fly with a particularly painful sting to torment her. Trying to escape from the fly, Io started running as fast as a cow is able to run. She ran the whole length of Greece from south to north, and did not stop when she came to a narrow neck of the sea between Europe and Asia. She plunged into the water, came ashore on the Asian side, and still kept running—leaving the neck of water with the new name Bosporus.

The Bosporus Bridge. This bridge completes the highway which enables motorists to drive from France to India.

The story does not say whether Io swam, or found a stretch of water that was shallow enough for wading. There is no such shallow stretch now but, in spite of the risk from strong, swift currents, swimming would certainly have been possible. In some places the Bosporus is only about half a mile (800 meters) wide.

Because of this small width, modern Istanbul has spilled across the Bosporus into Anatolia, the Asian part of Turkey. A

18

large and heavily loaded fleet of passenger and car ferries is constantly passing between the two shores. But the ferry loads have been growing lighter. There are now four bridges that span the Bosporus, the Atatürk, the Galata, the Fatih and the Bosporus bridges, providing direct road links between Istanbul and its Asian suburbs—and so, of course, between Turkey in Europe and Anatolia.

The Bosporus Bridge has also completed an international highway which allows motorists to drive all the way from the north coast of France to India. Between the bridge and the point where the road passes out of Turkey into Iran, they travel the whole 1,000-mile (1,600-kilometer) length of central Anatolia, and are therefore on the line of a much older "international highway"— perhaps the first long-distance land route used by man.

To the north, the south and the east, central Anatolia is walled by rugged and very high mountains. In the east, at the old volcano Mount Ararat, they rise to nearly 17,000 feet (5,168 meters). But the center itself is mainly plateau country—huge stretches of flat or rolling upland which make easy going for travelers on foot or on horseback—and travelers in early times were quick to take advantage of that. Right at the beginning of history, nomads, traders, armies, messengers, migrating peoples and even sightseers were using central Anatolia as a route to and from the further parts of Asia.

Many of these travelers settled along the route. In fact, it seems that the world's first farmers lived in Anatolia. They were nomads who came to gather the barley which grew wild in parts of the plateau, and at last learned how to get bigger crops by sowing seed and cultivating the plants. It seems likely too that Anatolia had the world's first metalworkers, house builders, and town dwellers. Archaeologists working on the plateau have found remains of towns which they believe to be at least 9,000 years old, much older than the earliest town remains found anywhere else.

If the archaeologists are right, it could well be that the very early history of man in Anatolia is hidden among the stories in the first book of the Bible. The Bible itself says that Noah's ark came to land near the top of Mount Ararat, and many scholars have thought that the Garden of Eden was the land between the upper reaches of the Tigris and Euphrates rivers, in southeastern Anatolia. That is the very place where—as it now seems—farming and metalwork started, and where some 9,000-year-old town remains have been found.

Of course, there is still no proof that the first book of the Bible tells of early Anatolia. However, it is worth remembering that in the Garden of Eden story Adam and Eve had a farmer son who built a town, and a great-grandson of a great-grandson who taught his people how to work metal. It is also interesting to find that copper—the first metal ever worked by man—is still mined near the Tigris River. Nowadays, this area is mined for other metals, too, and there are oil wells not very far away.

Whoever they were, the first farmers on the Anatolian plateau would have found the land and the climate much as

Anatolian goats. This herd is typical of those found in central Anatolia. The donkey in the foreground is the goat-herd's only means of transportation.

they are today—the climate hot in summer, sharply cold in winter, fairly dry all the year round; the land in most parts not very fertile, but good for grazing animals and growing grain crops. Perhaps the only major natural change has been the disappearance of trees. Some parts of the plateau are semi-desert by nature. There, trees have never grown. But other parts were well-wooded before the spread of people in need of fuel and goats in need of food. Recently, the Turkish government has been planting new forests, but people and goats are still a problem.

21

Goats and sheep are the main farm animals in central Anatolia. There are millions of both, and among the goats are many of the long-haired white breed which gives the fine, soft wool called mohair. This breed is native to Turkey. Its name, Angora, is an older way of spelling Ankara, the name of the capital city. To guard the flocks, there is also a large population of fierce and rather unfriendly dogs, often bigger than Alsatians. Many wear collars with sharp metal spikes to protect their throats if they are attacked by wolves. Cattle, donkeys and horses are the other common farm animals, while water buffaloes can often be seen at work where there is enough water to please them. So too can camels, where conditions are drier.

Most of these animals are also common on the coast lands of Anatolia and in European Turkey, but pigs are rarely kept anywhere. Nearly all the Turkish people are Muslims by religion. Most take the rules of their religion very seriously, and one rule is that they must not eat pork, bacon or any other pig meat.

Water buffaloes.

That helps to explain why there are still plenty of boar among Turkey's wild animals, but perhaps the main reason is that much of Turkey is still uncultivated and thinly populated. This allows room for wild animals which have died out in many parts of Europe—bears, for instance, and wolves, lynxes, and jackals. There are also some leopards. However, you are not likely to meet any leopards in European Turkey, or on the Anatolian coast lands. The few that are left live only in the remoter parts of Anatolia.

Like the Anatolian plateau, European Turkey is mainly grazing and grain-growing country, but the coast lands of Anatolia have richer soil and more rain than those areas, and can therefore grow a wider variety of crops. On the north coast, where the Pontic Mountains slope down to the Black Sea, the climate is temperate, with rain in all seasons of the year. These slopes are very well wooded, and the farmlands give large harvests of apples, stone fruits, and the hazelnuts which are one of Turkey's main exports. There are also tea and tobacco plantations.

In the west, where the coast land faces Greece across the Aegean Sea, the climate is of the type called Mediterranean. The winters are free of frost but rainy, the summers hot and dry, so this is an area of grapes and oranges and lemons, of melons and olives and figs. The dried figs exported from Smyrna (now called Izmir) have been famous for centuries. Cotton too is grown on the southern half of the Aegean coast. It was from here that the first cotton used in Britain was exported during the reign of the first Queen Elizabeth.

Around the corner, on the south-facing lands below the Taurus Mountains where we began, the climate is still Mediterranean, but warmer all the year round. Here, the temperature is usually above 50 degrees Fahrenheit (10 degrees Celsius) in winter, and can rise to more than 100 degrees Fahrenheit (38 degrees Celsius) in the summer. In these conditions, farmers can be very successful with such crops as sugarcane, bananas and dates—crops which usually like to be a little nearer the tropics than an area north of latitude 36 degrees. Of course, the farmers on this coast can also grow all the more usual Mediterranean crops which are grown on the coast facing the Aegean Sea.

From that brief glance over the whole of Turkey, you may have guessed that the Turks are mainly a farming people. About four in every ten of them live by growing crops or grazing animals, and about one-third of the value of Turkey's exports comes from the produce of its farms and pastures. The farms are usually small—about 10 acres (less than four hectares) in area and sometimes very much less. Many are also broken up into small fields widely scattered, which makes them hard to work, and not so productive as they could be. As a result, about half the farmers of Turkey need to have more land before they can reach the living standard of the average farmer in western Europe. Luckily for them, the land is there, and in recent years the government has been gradually giving more of it to the farmers who need it most. Some has also been going to new farmers—people who have come back to Turkey after spending a few years in western Europe as industrial workers, or people of Turkish blood who have come to Turkey as refugees after losing their homes in other countries.

For some of Turkey's people, this has been putting an end to a way of life that is as old as Turkey's history. These people are nomads—tent-dwelling herders who graze their animals over high ground while the summer lasts, and drive them down to lower, warmer pastures when the winter draws near. Until the government began giving more land to settled farmers, there was usually plenty of pasture for the nomads wherever they moved, but now there is less and less of it. Many nomads have

A Kurdish encampment. These people are tent-dwelling nomads.

found that the only way they can live is to become settled farmers themselves, and the government is encouraging them to do so. However, those who are trying to keep up the nomadic way of life are not being treated harshly, as they are in some other countries. Perhaps that is because the settled people remember that the original Turks were nomads—nomads who arrived in Anatolia hardly a 1,000 years ago, bringing their Muslim religion and the Turkish language with them.

Little by little, they had come a long way, perhaps 2,000 miles (3,200 kilometers), from their desert homeland near the center of Asia. There, they had lived as a tribe of horse-riding warriors, strong, brave, proud, careless of hardship and hunger, willing to do what they were told by leaders whom they respected, rather lazy in good times but hard workers when they had to be, and always ready to fight for pastures that could not be had or held peaceably. It was their power as fighting men which brought them through the hazards of their journey from Central Asia, and gave them a new and more comfortable homeland in Anatolia.

A visitor need not be in Turkey long to find that some of these characteristics are still noticeable in the Turks of today, but he will also find that another characteristic of the original Turk has almost completely disappeared. Like most central Asian people, the original Turks were rather more Chinese than European in appearance, but people of that type are rarely seen in Turkey nowadays. If a modern Turk were to visit central Asia, he would almost certainly be taken for a European.

26

This man (photographed outside a mosque in Istanbul) has typical Turkish features.

Indeed he might well be taken for a Greek in Greece, or an Italian in southern Italy. Some might even be taken for Germans in Germany, as there are fair-haired, blue-eyed Turks among the more usual darker types. The most well-known Turk of modern times belonged to the fair type. He was Mustafa Kemal (later known as Kemal Atatürk), a great soldier and statesman who became the first president of the Turkish Republic.

To understand why the Turks of today look so different from the nomads who founded their nation, we must first take a look at Turkey before the Turks.

27

2

Turkey Before the Turks

Of course, there was no Turkey before the Turks if we think of names only. The name Turkey—or *Türkiye* as it is spelled in Turkish—came *after* the Turks, not before them. But we are not thinking of a name. We are thinking of a country as the homeland of human beings, and in that sense Turkey was already very old when the Turks arrived there, perhaps as old as the human race, and almost certainly as old as the beginnings of human civilization. The towns of 8,000 and 9,000 years ago which have been found on the Anatolian plateau were not new towns even then. Utensils, tools and ornaments uncovered by archaeologists—as well as the buildings themselves—show the needs, knowledge, and skills of a people already civilized for many centuries.

Unfortunately, there is nothing to tell us who these people were, or even what they looked like. They left no writing, nor any clear pictures of themselves in the wall paintings that decorated some of their main buildings.

Little more is known of the many other people who settled in

Threshing, in Anatolia. Some of the world's first-known farming settlements were in this region.

Anatolia or passed through Anatolia over the next 3,000 years. The museums of Turkey, and of many other countries, are well stocked with things that these peoples made and used—pottery, metalwork, tools, sculpture, weapons—and from some of the designs and decoration we can learn a little about their gods and their religious ideas. However, there are very few leads to their other ideas, or to their history, their languages, and their true physical appearance. All that we can safely say is that by the year 2000 B.C. the Anatolians must have been a very mixed people, mainly with brownish skin and dark hair; a people who

29

**This relief from
Ankara shows typical
Hittite features
which are still noticeable
in some Turks.**

spoke languages that are now mostly forgotten, and who lived as peaceful farmers and herders when new invaders allowed them to do so. Many were ruled by kings whose kingdoms were no bigger than a single town with the land and mud-brick villages around it, and the little that we know of them comes mainly from the uncovered ruins of such towns.

We know a great deal more about two other peoples who were to be the next invaders. These were the Assyrians, and the Hittites—both often mentioned in Bible stories. The Hittites had been nomads. They came from a large group of fair-skinned tribes which had been spreading from the lands north of the Black Sea into other parts of Europe, and also into Asia. Nowadays, we call the whole group the Indo-Europeans, because their language was the ancestor of nearly every language now spoken in Europe, and of many languages spoken in India and countries near India.

On the other hand, the Assyrians were a settled Asian people. Clever and civilized but very warlike, they were building up a powerful state to the south of Anatolia, and needed copper to make bronze for their tools and weapons. That brought them into Anatolia itself, where they founded colonies in the copper-mining areas. The colonists made permanent homes, intermarrying with the local people, and they might have spread more widely if the Indo-European Hittites had not started moving in from the northeast.

The Hittites had also come to stay, but they were not content to settle in small colonies. They took over the whole of central Anatolia, and set themselves up as a ruling class over the rest of the people. If we can judge by their writings, they ruled well and fairly. They also defended the country so strongly that other invaders were held off for about six hundred years, though peaceful immigrants were still allowed room to settle. Some of these immigrants would have used a fine road that the Hittites built to help in defending and developing the country. It crossed the whole of Anatolia from east to west—more than 3,000 years before the modern highway was planned.

When the Hittites lost power at last, they lost it to other Indo-Europeans—mainly Greeks and other Greek-speaking peoples. The Greeks—or the Hellenes as they called themselves—had begun moving into Greece at about the same time as the Hittites moved into Anatolia. Like the Hittites, they were moving into a country that was already inhabited, and some of the inhabitants—a small, dark people—fled across the

31

Aegean Sea to the Anatolian coast lands. There, near the southern entrance to the Sea of Marmara, they found yet more Indo-European invaders: a community now known as the Trojans. The Trojans had set up a kingdom around a very ancient Anatolian city named Troy, and had become very well-known as horsebreeders. As they grew more powerful, they also tried to control and tax the sea-traffic passing between the Aegean Sea and the Sea of Marmara. This put them on bad terms with the Greeks on the European side of the Aegean, and led to the most famous war in history the Trojan War, in which the Greeks were able to sack Troy because the Trojans had found an enormous wooden horse outside the city gates, and could not resist taking it into the city. They had not thought that its inside might be packed tight with Greek soldiers.

Legend says that the war began because a Trojan prince had stolen Helen, the wife of a Greek king. That could possibly be true, but war would certainly have come even if Helen had stayed at home. No country likes to feel that another country could block its ships and the supplies that they carry—and this remains a problem for modern Turkey.

After the Trojan War, Greeks began to settle along the west coast of Anatolia. At the same time, their kinsmen the Phrygians were pushing inland, and at last drove the Hittites back to the mountains in the east. There, the Hittites gradually disappeared as a separate people. However, their looks did not disappear. Even today, many Turks have faces very much

Among the remains of ancient civilizations in Turkey is this head of Apollo—once part of a gigantic statue of the god. He is wearing a Phrygian cap.

like the faces in the realistic sculpture that the Hittites left behind them.

As for the Phrygians, they too lost their power at last, and disappeared in the Anatolian mixture of peoples. Now, they are best remembered for inventing a type of pointed cloth headgear called the Phrygian cap, and by stories of their most famous king, Midas. One story tells how Midas was granted the wish that everything he touched would turn to gold—and was very

33

soon wishing that it would not. In another story, the god Apollo punishes Midas by turning his ears into donkeys ears.

The stories are fiction, of course, but perhaps the one about gold grew from the fact that there was plenty of gold to be taken from the rocks and rivers of western Anatolia when the Phrygians were the ruling people. Certainly the Lydians who followed them became very prosperous from trading in gold. They also made gold coins, and indeed were the first people to make and use true coins of any metal. So it seems no wonder that the last of their kings, Croesus, was thought to be the richest man who had ever lived.

These Lydians, another people related to the Greeks, also gained power over the Greek colonies on the western coast of Anatolia. Less civilized than the Greeks, they used Greek craftsmen to improve their main city, Sardis, and Greek soldiers to strengthen their army. In return, they taught the Greeks some new ideas which were later taken to Europe—for instance, games with dice and knucklebones, the use of scent, and a musical scale called the Lydian mode, which is still often heard in folk and church music.

The Lydians, and the Phrygians before them, had stopped the Greek colonists from spreading their settlements inland. But the whole long coastline was open to them, and by the sixth century before Christ there were Greek colonies all around it, and on many of the offshore islands. The colonies were independent of each other, each governing itself as a separate city-state. Many became more prosperous and more advanced in civilization than the city-states of Greece itself, and from them came some of the greatest of the ancient Greek thinkers, sculptors, scientists, writers, and architects. Nowadays, it is often forgotten that men as great as Homer the poet, Pythagoras the mathematician, and Democritus the first atomic scientist were not European Greeks, but Greeks born and bred in what is now Turkey. Though less far from their "motherland," these Anatolian Greeks were no more closely connected with it than modern Americans and Australians are connected with the British Isles.

Nor could the "motherland" protect their independence when the whole of Anatolia was taken by Persian invaders in 546 B.C. It was all that the European Greeks could do to protect their own independence. At the southern entrance to the Sea of Marmara, the Persians tied a line of boats about one mile (16 kilometers) long across the strait called the Hellespont, and used it as a bridge to invade Europe. There, the Greeks managed to drive them back across the water, but no further. The Persians remained the rulers of all Anatolia for more than two centuries.

By then, the European Greeks had become united under the king of a neighboring country, Alexander the Great of Macedonia. Alexander had dreams of winning a great empire, and in 334 B.C. he set out to make them come true. With a large Greek army he crossed the Hellespont, drove the Persians out of Anatolia, and went on to conquer Persia (now Iran) itself.

Anatolia then became mainly a Greek country, and it remained so even when three tribes of Celts from Europe invaded the plateau, and when the newly powerful Romans took over the government of the whole country. The Celtic invaders were the people called Galatians in the Bible. They were related to the Celts of the British Isles and other parts of western Europe, and spoke a language rather like Welsh. No one in Turkey speaks their language now, but some people still say that they can see Celtic features among the Turks who live in the district around Ankara, where most of the Galatians lived.

Unlike the Galatians, the Romans did not come to Anatolia as settlers. They came as soldiers protecting the boundaries of the Roman Empire against invaders, as officials making money for the Roman government by taxing the Anatolians, and as businessmen making money for themselves by using the country's natural resources. However, there were some gains for the Anatolians, too. Under Roman protection, they could live in peace; and with Roman skills in building and engineering, life in their towns at least became healthier and much more comfortable.

Also under the Romans, Anatolia had a new kind of "invader"—the first missionaries of the Christian religion. They came from the birthplace of Christianity (now Israel) to the south of Anatolia, and among them was the apostle Saint Paul. Saint Paul had a special interest in converting the Anatolians. Though Jewish by ancestry, he was an Anatolian himself, born in the city of Tarsus. Tarsus, near the eastern end of the south

A painting of the original Santa Claus, bishop of Myra.

coast, is still a busy little city; but the birthplace of another famous Christian of Anatolia has almost disappeared. This is Patara, an old Roman seaport at the other end of the south coast. The famous Christian born here was Saint Nicholas, who became bishop of Myra, a neighboring city which has been replaced by a modern town named Demre. In Myra, Saint Nicholas was well-known for his kindness to children, and because of that he is now well-known everywhere under the Dutch form of his name—Santa Claus.

There were three hundred years between Saint Paul and Saint Nicholas, and during those centuries Christianity became the main religion of the Anatolians. It also, in 330 A.D., became the official religion of the whole Roman Empire. By then, the Roman Empire was in trouble. Rebellions and invasions were making it difficult to govern from Rome, the capital city. So the Emperor Constantine decided to have a new capital in the eastern half of the empire. He chose a small city in Thrace, a Greek-speaking country to the north of Greece. The city was Byzantion—Byzantium in the Latin language of the Roman Empire. It lay on the western shore of the Bosporus, and had a fine natural harbor, the Golden Horn, which opened into the Bosporus.

Byzantium became the center of the Roman Empire in 330 A.D., and in honor of Constantine it was given the new name Constantinopolis, which in Greek means Constantine's City. In English, the name was shortened to Constantinople, and the Turks have shortened it so much more that it is hard to recognize Istanbul as an abbreviation. However, the older name Byzantium lingered for many centuries, and the empire ruled from the city is still remembered as the Byzantine Empire.

For a time, the Italian city of Rome remained a second capital, with a second emperor ruling the western half of the empire. But after 476 A.D. there was no Roman Empire in the west. It had broken up into small, badly-governed, and sometimes ungoverned fragments, often fighting among themselves and against invaders from the north. For western Europe, this was the beginning of the centuries called the Dark Ages.

About the same time, a dark age began for Anatolia. While Byzantium grew huge and rich and strong, Anatolia's towns and cities were not allowed to develop, or to behave independently. The emperors were afraid that strong, prosperous cities might become rivals to Byzantium, and perhaps centers of rebellion. As for the farmland, most of that was turned into huge estates for friends and relations of the emperors, and worked by people who were almost slaves. The emperors were also very harsh with people who, though Christians, could not agree with all the beliefs of the official Christian church. So perhaps it is not surprising that, as time went on, the Anatolians grew rather half-hearted about helping the empire to guard its borders. That is one reason why some nomads from central Asia managed to spread through Anatolia between 1063 and 1073 A.D. Another reason was that when the emperor brought an army to drive them back they beat it soundly. They also captured the emperor himself; and then their leader Alp Arslan sent him shamefully but safely back to Byzantium.

There, he was not so lucky. He found that he had lost his throne to a rival, and he soon lost his life, too. The rival could do little to stop the nomad invaders. He had enough trouble in other parts of the empire, and also in Byzantium itself. So Alp Arslan—Alp the Lion—became the real ruler of Anatolia. He and his nomads were the first Turks in Turkey.

3

Alp to Atatürk

Alp Arslan and his nomads were not new to the ways of civilization. They belonged to a Turkish tribe called the Seljuks, who had moved into Persia (Iran) before they thought of Anatolia. At that time, around 1030 A.D., Persia was still a powerful country, and a very advanced one. In the arts and sciences, only Byzantium could rival it. Also, it was a much bigger country than it is today. Within its boundaries lay the city of Baghdad, then the magnificent city of the Arabian Nights stories, and the seat of the Caliph, the head of the Muslim religion.

The Seljuks adapted very well to such different surroundings—so well that one of their leaders became chief guard to the Caliph and then, with the title Sultan, the real ruler of the country. His son, Alp Arslan, also became Sultan, and so ruled both Persia and Anatolia, but after Alp died Anatolia became independent, with a Seljuk sultan of its own.

The Seljuk rulers saw Anatolia as their own country, and not—like the Byzantines—as a place from which they could

The tomb of one of the early sultans. The decorated tiles are an example of a craft introduced by the Seljuks.

take endless supplies of food and raw materials, and give little in return. So Anatolia grew prosperous again, both from its old occupations and from two new ones brought in by the Seljuks. These were the crafts of weaving carpets and making decorated tiles, both of which remain important in modern Turkey. Building too began again under the Seljuks, often with skills and in styles that the Seljuks had learned in Persia. Some of the most beautiful mosques (Muslim churches) and other town buildings now to be seen in Turkey go back to Seljuk times.

However, there was more to Seljuk Anatolia than fine buildings and thriving industries. Perhaps surprisingly, if you think that the idea of a welfare state is a modern one, the Seljuk government provided the people with free medical treatment, hospitals, and many other social services. It even went one better than the modern welfare state: there was free accommodations for all travelers, including tourists—very comfortable accommodations, too.

The Seljuks were also very tolerant of other people's religious beliefs. Under the first Seljuk sultans, most Anatolians were still Christians, and they were allowed to remain so, without persecution or interference. It was not until Christian Crusaders from western Europe began using Anatolia as a through road to Jerusalem in the Holy Land that religious troubles began. The Crusaders were trying to recapture Jerusalem from the Muslims who held it, and some tried to recapture parts of Anatolia for Byzantium on the way. That led to battles between Seljuks and Crusaders, and it made the Seljuk rulers suspicious of the Anatolian Christians. It also brought the Byzantines back to parts of Anatolia, and made many Anatolian Christians change their religion, or at any rate let their children grow up as Muslims. By the time the Crusades were over, the Anatolians were almost wholly a Muslim people.

Partly because they had to keep a close watch on the Crusaders, the Seljuks could not keep new waves of nomads out of eastern Anatolia, nor control them when they settled.

42

The Ottoman sultan who conquered Constantinople in 1453.

Many of these were Turks from other tribes, and some became strong, independent communities, often at war with each other or in rebellion against the Seljuks when they were not attacking the few parts of Anatolia that were still held by Byzantium.

It was one of these groups, led by a man named Othman, which at last replaced the Seljuks as rulers of Anatolia. Othman (whose name is spelled and pronounced Osman in modern Turkish) founded a line of sultans which lasted from before 1300 to 1922. He also gave his name to one of the world's great empires, the Ottoman or Osmanli Empire.

Unlike the Seljuks, Othman and his successors were not content to stay in Asia. Before Anatolia was completely in their hands, they crossed to Europe, and captured most of

43

Thrace (the country around the Byzantine capital, Constantinople). Constantinople was too strong for them to take just yet, but they made a cunning move towards taking it. By changing their own capital from Bursa in Anatolia to Edirne in the west of Thrace, they cut Constantinople off from much of the Byzantine Empire in Europe.

That part of the Byzantine Empire was made up mainly of the countries that are now called Romania, Bulgaria, Yugoslavia, and Albania. All these soon fell to the Ottomans, and became part of the new Ottoman Empire. Greece fell, too,

The Mosque of Sultan Ahmed (Blue Mosque), Istanbul. The Ottomans made the city the capital of their Muslim empire.

and before the conquest was complete Constantinople had fallen. In 1458, it replaced Edirne as the capital of Ottoman Turkey; and, with the name of Istanbul, it remained the capital until Ankara replaced it in 1920.

The Ottomans did not give up empire-building when they had taken Constantinople. In Europe, their territory spread to the borders of Austria and into the parts of Russia along the northern shores of the Black Sea. In Asia, they took all of Arabia, and everything west of Iran. In Africa, the whole of the north from Egypt to Algeria came under the star and crescent flag of Turkey. So too did the large islands of Crete and Cyprus, and many small islands in the Aegean and Mediterranean Seas.

The sultans of Turkey could not make their empire any bigger, but from the reign of Sultan Selim I (1512-1520) they had an influence on a great many people who lived far beyond the empire's boundaries. Sultan Selim became Caliph (head of the Muslim religion) as well as the head of the Ottoman empire, and so he and the sultans who followed him could claim the religious allegiance of Muslims everywhere.

Within the Muslim empire, the Ottomans were usually as tolerant of Christians as the Seljuks had been. If the sultan's Christian subjects obeyed the laws and respected the Muslim religion, they were allowed to live without harm and without much discrimination. Many Christian men reached high positions in their sultan's service, and many Muslim men—including several sultans—married Christian women.

However, the Ottomans could be very harsh in their treatment of people taken prisoner during their many wars with Christian countries. Men, women, and children were treated as slaves, and sometimes forced to become Muslims. Strong and healthy boys were also forced into schooling as recruits for the janissaries—a regiment of highly-trained soldiers who were the sultan's palace guard and the shock troops of his army. It was the janissaries who led the conquests that made the Ottoman Empire. They were feared and famous everywhere for their disciplined fury in battle. And one of them, nicknamed Skander Beg (Lord Alexander) was also famous for refusing to fight his own people, the Albanians. Instead, he changed sides, and led the Albanians against the Turks.

There were very few men like Skander Beg among the janissaries. Most had been trained so hard and for so long that they were "brainwashed," and would only fight as they were told to fight. But as time went on the wars of conquest ended. Turkey's empire had spread as far as it could go, and the powerful sultans who made it were followed by weaker rulers. The training of the janissaries slackened. So too did their loyalty to the sultans, and the sultans now found that they could not control their own guards. Before long, the janissaries were trying to control the sultans, and rioting when they could not have their own way. More than once, they set fire to parts of Istanbul and, in 1807, they murdered Sultan Selim III who was trying to disband them.

The next sultan, Mahmud II, did disband them, and very

46

violently. When they rioted he called other soldiers to suppress the riot, and after a last battle very few janissaries were left. But by then Turkey had other troubles. The Greeks were fighting successfully for independence. Other parts of the empire were beginning to break away. And many of the Turks themselves were dissatisfied with the state of their country. They wanted a greater share in the government than the sultan had allowed them.

These felt that in science, industry, and civilization, Turkey was going backwards while western Europe was going forward.

That was especially so in Anatolia. The Ottoman sultans had always been more interested in Europe than in Asia, and had treated Anatolia in much the same way as the Byzantine emperors had treated it. The country had been neglected, misgoverned, and exploited for centuries. All the achievements of the Seljuk sultans had been lost. There was no concern for the welfare of the people. On the roads, where there had once been free accommodation for travelers, it was hard to make an hour's journey without attacks from bandits or uncontrolled invading nomads. And if Anatolians crossed the Bosporus to seek a better living in and around Constantinople, they found themselves in competition with the many people from the European parts of the empire who had already settled there.

Those Europeans were the last reason why so few of the modern Turkish people have the central Asian features of the nomads who founded their nation. When the first Turks came to what is now Turkey, they found there a people who, after thousands of years of mixing, looked much like the Mediterranean peoples of today. With those, the Turks mixed again, to make a new people whose features were still Mediterranean rather than central Asian. And then, in the centuries of the Ottoman Empire, this people mixed widely with people from all over Europe—citizens of Greece, Romania, and the other empire countries, captives and settlers from as far north as Britain and Scandinavia. In this mixture, the central Asian features of the first Turks were almost lost, so that the typical 20th-century Turk is a European-looking Turk, even if he lives as far into Asia as Mount Ararat.

Among the many people from other nations who became Turks in Ottoman times were the ancestors of a boy named Mustafa, who was born in 1881. Mustafa had no other name, but that was not unusual. Until the 1930s, Turks did not have family names. However, Mustafa's schoolwork was so good that one of his teachers gave him the nickname Kemal, which means *perfect*. And as Turks sometimes used a nickname as a kind of surname, Mustafa grew up as Mustafa Kemal.

Like many young Turks of his time—and also many older ones—Mustafa Kemal wanted to see a new Turkey, with a government, laws, civil rights, and services like those in the countries of western Europe. There was nothing original in that. People had been talking about a new Turkey all through the 19th century. But it was only talk. And while the talk went on, conditions in the Ottoman countries grew so much worse that among foreigners Turkey became known as "the sick man of Europe."

Some foreigners also thought that the only way to cure "the sick man" was to take control of him. That led to the Crimean War (1853-1856) in which Britain and France joined the Turks in a struggle to keep Russia out of Turkey. Russia was kept out, but the health of Turkey did not improve. The country grew poorer as more and more of its wealth went to foreigners. There was always rebellion in one part of the empire or another—and sometimes in several parts at once. A sultan who tried to give the Turks a more democratic form of government, better education, and a higher standard of living was murdered by people who wanted to keep Turkey as it was. The next sultan went mad. The next agreed to govern more democratically, but almost at once went back on his agreement and turned the country into a police state.

It was in that police state that Mustafa Kemal grew up, became an army officer, and began to take an interest in his country's future. About the same time, a number of other young men formed a political society called the Young Turks. It was a secret society at first, much persecuted by the police, but it soon had so much support that it was able to defy the sultan and put him off his throne.

Through the next sultan, the Young Turks were able to force improvements in government, and many of the other reforms that people had wanted for so long. But they made two mistakes. By making enemies of the remaining parts of the empire, they caused a war which left Turkey with only one small part of Europe—the city of Istanbul and the country around it. Then they took Turkey into the First World War on the side of Germany, and so lost the rest of the Ottoman Empire.

Mustafa Kemal did not like the idea of an alliance with Germany. He would rather have kept with Turkey's older friends, Britain and France. But, as an army officer, he obeyed orders, fought against the British and their allies in the famous Gallipoli campaign, and led the Turkish troops who stopped them from taking Istanbul.

That did not prevent the Turks and their German allies from losing the war, and the rest of the Ottoman Empire. The Turks then found that they were also likely to lose some of Turkey itself. In the peace treaty, the sultan agreed to let the Greeks and the Armenians have parts of Anatolia as separate countries. But General Mustafa Kemal got there before them. In defiance of the sultan he went to Anatolia, organized an army, and pushed back the Greeks and the Armenians. Neither Britain nor France tried to stop him. Nor did the sultan. He had too much support from his countrymen.

Mustafa Kemal's countrymen also supported him when he formed the Grand National Assembly—a parliament—in Ankara to take over the government from the sultan in Istanbul. The sultan was dethroned. On October 29, 1923, Mustafa Kemal was elected president of the new Turkish republic.

The main aim of the new government was to modernize Turkey—to reshape it as far as possible on the lines of the nations of western Europe. Among many more important changes, it was decided that every Turk must choose and use a surname. But Mustafa Kemal did not have to make a choice. Because he had held the Turks together through a very difficult time, and given them the chance of a better future, they gave him the surname Atatürk, which means *Father of the Turks*. So Mustafa, who became Mustafa Kemal, had another change of name and became Kemal Atatürk.

Now let us look at life in the republic which Kemal Atatürk founded.

4

In Turkey Today

If someone who had lived in Turkey before 1923 were to go back now, his biggest surprise would be the sight of so many bare-headed men and bare-faced women. Before 1923, a Turkish woman rarely left her house without putting a veil over her face, and a Turkish man usually covered his head with a fez—a stiff red cap, shaped like a flowerpot turned upside down. But in Turkey today it is the veiled woman who is a rarity, and men who are not bare-headed usually wear ordinary European hats and caps. The fez is not worn at all. In fact, it is against the law for a Turk to wear one.

Kemal Atatürk's new government discouraged the veil and forbade the fez partly because it believed that Turkey could have a better future if the people became more like Europeans in their behavior and their ideas. Many Turks thought that the government had no right to interfere with their choice of clothing, and objected strongly. There were even riots against the new law. However, most people obeyed willingly enough. The Turks have gradually given up wearing some other traditional

Traditional Turkish dress, plus a modern cardigan and glasses.

Turkish clothes; for instance, the various types of baggy trousers which had been worn by both men and women. Nowadays, it is only on festive occasions or in country places that such clothes are seen, though many women who no longer wear veils have not given up the reason for wearing them. They wear large headscarves instead, and cover their faces with the corners when they are near strange men.

The veil and the fez were symbols of the Muslim religion. So, in getting rid of them, the government was not only trying to make the Turks look and feel more European. It was also trying to show them—and the world—that the Muslim religion was no longer a state religion, as it had been in Ottoman times. That does not mean that the Muslim religion was banned, nor even that the government was against it. Most members of the government were Muslim themselves, as were 98 out of every 100 other Turks. But when the sultan was also the caliph, Muslim leaders had been very powerful. They had interfered in government, influenced the law, controlled education, and kept the country clinging to many ideas and customs which, to people with western ideas, seemed backward and sometimes unjust. For instance, women had very little freedom, and very few rights. It was even possible for a man to divorce his wife simply by telling her to go away.

Kemal Atatürk and his supporters did not want that in the new Turkey. Nor did they want any distinction between Muslims and people of other religions, as there had been in Ottoman times. Then, people of other religions were not citi-

Muslims at prayer in a mosque.

zens in the eyes of the law, although Christians and Jews were otherwise treated tolerantly. So Turkey became—as it is today—a country in which the Muslim religion has no special privileges, and no influence on the government.

Most Muslims were ready to accept the change, but the change did not affect their religious beliefs. About 99 in every 100 Turks are still Muslims, and in any Turkish town the tall, thin minarets (pointed towers) of mosques are still the main feature of the skyline.

Because so many Turks remain Muslims, daily life in Turkey has not become wholly westernized. Five times each day a voice—often over a loudspeaker—cries: "There is no god but God, and Muhammad is his prophet." That is the call to prayer, and five times each day good Muslims answer it by stopping to pray, whatever they are doing and wherever they are.

For a whole month of each year, the month called Ramadan, all good Muslims will neither eat nor drink between sunrise

This inscription in a museum in Istanbul is a reminder of the importance the Arabic language once held in Turkey.

and sunset. Children are not expected to fast so severely, but that makes them no less hungry at the end of Ramadan, when there are three days called Şeker Bayrami, which means "Sugar Holiday." For Muslims, these days are something like Christmas. There is also much feasting and giving of presents over the days of the Festival of Sacrifices, about three months after Ramadan.

Unlike Christmas, these festivals have no fixed dates on the modern calendar. Nor does Ramadan. For religious purposes, Muslims use an old calendar whose year is 11 days shorter than the modern calendar year. Therefore, events which are timed by the old calendar come 11 days earlier in each year of the modern calendar. For example, if Ramadan begins on

August 28th in 1976, it will begin on August 17th in 1977, August 6th in 1978, and so on.

The old Muslim calendar was once the only calendar used in Turkey. But even in Ottoman times the Turks were more closely connected with Europe than they were with other Muslim countries, and they found it very confusing to deal with people who used a calendar so different from their own. So the Ottoman sultans at last began to change to the modern calendar. The change was completed by Kemal Atatürk's government, when it made Sunday the weekly day of rest instead of the Muslim Friday. However, even though Friday is now a working day, large numbers of Muslims still find time for midday prayers in a mosque.

The Turkish language has also changed since Ottoman times. When the Muslim religion spread from Arabia to other

A street in Izmir. Note the signs in the Latin alphabet with additional Turkish letters and accents.

countries, the Arabic language went with it. So, wherever he lived, and whatever his native tongue, a Muslim had to know some Arabic before he could read the Koran (the Muslim Bible) and understand the prayers in mosques. Often too he had to know Arabic to get some general education. Because of this, many Arabic words came into the Turkish language, sometimes replacing Turkish words in the same way as, for some English-speaking people, the French word *hotel* has replaced the English word *inn*.

For the same reason, the Seljuk and Ottoman Turks used the Arabic alphabet for writing their own language. However, the Arabic alphabet is not a good one for writing Turkish. It has no letters for many Turkish sounds, and it has several letters for which there are no Turkish sounds. It is also hard to learn and to write clearly. As Kemal Atatürk's government wanted the Turks to be a better-educated people, it decided that Turkey must have a new alphabet. For the new one, it chose the Latin alphabet of western Europe—the alphabet in which this book is printed—with some extra letters which make it easier for Turks to learn and use.

The extra letters were made by putting the small marks ', ¨ and ˘ over or under some of the old letters, and by using an *i* without a dot as well as an *i* with one. For example, *ş* has the sound *sh*, *ö* the sound of the *u* in *burn* or the *ea* in *learn*, *ğ* the sound of the *y* in *yes*, and *ı* the sound of the second *o* in *London*. So the ordinary English sounds of the words *Merton's shop* would be written *Mötin's şop*.

A secondary school chemistry lesson.

The government gave the whole country exactly three months to learn and start using the new alphabet, and everybody who knew it was set to teaching some of those who did not. Kemal Atatürk himself gave public lessons. At the same time, teachers and government officials were told that they must stop using Arabic and other foreign words wherever there were old Turkish words to replace them. That was less easy than changing the alphabet, but the Turkish language is now much more Turkish than it was in Ottoman times, even though it still has many foreign words. These include some English ones like *coach, football,* and *international*—spelled *koç, futbol,* and *enternasyonal.*

When the new alphabet was introduced, only a small minority of Turks knew the old one. Very few children went to school, and many of those who did go went for only a short time—often less than a year. With the new alphabet came a plan for free and compulsory education, in a state education system similar to those of western Europe. The plan has been working out steadily, but slowly. The compulsory school leaving age is 14, though many children leave earlier. Some still do not go to

59

Anatolian peasants.

school at all. However, children who do stay until they are 14 may go on to free secondary education, and that can give them the chance of a place at one of the 19 universities.

Turkey's education plans have been slow to work out mainly because so many of the people live in rural villages. There are more than 40,000 of these villages, and most of them are small, out-of-the-way places with very few comforts or amusements. Often there is not even a shop, and many villages are still waiting for electricity. Such conditions are not very attractive to most teachers. They would much rather have the convenience and comfort of town life, and so village children must sometimes go without a teacher, even though there are now more primary schools than there are villages.

Generally, village people are poorer on the plateau than on the coast lands. Of those who live on the plateau, the easterners are poorer than the westerners. However, a village house anywhere rarely has more than two rooms; in many villages every house has only one. Sometimes, a house is no more than a man-made cave, a single room hollowed out of a hillside or rock. But most houses are made of mud bricks, and so are the same color as the local soil—usually brown, greyish-brown, or yellowish-brown. This often makes them hard to see, even from a fairly short distance. As a result, motorists and train travelers crossing the plateau sometimes have the impression that it is almost uninhabited. Many houses have no window; of those which do have a window, the opening is covered with a goatskin more often than with glass.

Food is usually cooked over a fire-hole dug in the earth floor of the house, or outside near the doorway. Except in areas which are still forested, or where coal mines are handy, the fuel is dried dung.

The occupants of a village house—often a large number for its size—usually take their food from a tray on the floor, or on a platform which stands a little above the floor. They also sleep on the floor, using mattresses which are rolled up during the

61

day, to make more room. In fact, home life for many village Turks is very much like life in the tents of the nomads who were their ancestors. Also like those tents, village houses are always kept tidy and very clean, and nearly all of them contain a carpet that is well-made and beautiful.

For Muslim Turks, the carpet is not only a useful household article that may also be the only decorative household article. It is a religious article, too. People kneel and pray on it when they are in the house at any of the five daily prayer times. Many Muslims also have smaller, lighter carpets which they carry with them and use for praying when they are away from home. These are the prayer rugs which visitors sometimes buy.

Carpets are equally a feature of houses in Turkish towns, but otherwise there is little similarity between the average town house and the average village house. Generally, townspeople in Turkey have a higher standard of living than country people, Turkish towns have houses and apartments in all the sizes and styles seen in western Europe—and with all the variety of furniture and furnishings. However, very few town houses are furnished and equipped as well as the homes of town workers in western countries. The wages and salaries of most Turkish townspeople are still much lower than they are in the west.

Also, the cities and some of the larger towns have a growing number of people who find it difficult to pay for a home of any kind. These are people who have moved in from the country hoping for better-paid work in the factory industries, but have found no work at all, or perhaps a little part-time work.

Luckily for some of them, there is one way out of the difficulty. If a man can find a small piece of land without an owner, and build a house on it in a single night, an ancient Turkish law allows him to live there permanently. As it happens, there is still a good deal of ownerless land, so many unemployed people have been taking advantage of the law. Of course, a house built in a single night can be little more than a shack. And where many such houses are built close together they can easily become a slum. To that problem, the government has not yet found an answer.

It is not only the hope of better-paid work that brings these people away from the country areas. It is also the amusements that town life can offer. There is very little entertainment in the rural villages of Turkey, especially the smaller ones. In many there is nothing but the teahouse—usually for men only—where customers sit for hours sipping milkless tea or water sweetened with jam, and perhaps puffing a "hubblebubble" pipe, as they play backgammon. Some villages have a public radio or television set for the many people who cannot afford one of their own. A very big village may have a cinema. And that is all, except for folk-dancing on special occasions, and a rare visit by a traveling show—perhaps some wrestling camels or other performing animals, or a shadow play with puppets. The shadow plays are usually about a comic character called Karagöz (Black Eye), who is something like Punch in a Punch and Judy show. Karagöz and similar puppet plays may be seen in towns

A detail from a Turkish carpet. Turkish carpets are well-made and very decorative.

and cities, too—but much less frequently since the spread of cinemas and the beginning of the Turkish television service.

Soccer, played all year round, is very popular in the towns, and for townspeople who prefer a more traditional Turkish sport there are always wrestling matches. Turkish wrestlers are known in stadiums all around the world, and have won Olympic Games medals. However, true Turkish wrestling is rarely seen outside Turkey. In that form of the sport, the contestants make it harder for each other to get a grip by covering their bodies with oil.

In Turkey, even when their incomes are fairly low, towns people also have a wider variety of food than many country

64

people. Rural Turkey produces very good meat, and some of the best fruit and vegetables in the world, but most of these products go to town markets. So it is mainly in towns that the visitor sees people eating western-style steaks, and such traditional Turkish meat dishes as *şiş kebab* and *şişköfte*—cubes of meat or balls of mincemeat, both grilled on skewers, often with pieces of onion, tomato, or some other vegetable between them.

The poorer country people and there are millions of them—eat fresh meat only on special occasions like the Festival of Sacrifices, or when bad seasons make them kill animals which would otherwise die of hunger. In ordinary times, their main food is bread made from their own grain, with whatever else they can produce for themselves—onions, perhaps, and goat's milk cheese and, in some areas, a strongly spiced dried meat called *pastirma*. Under the name pastrami, *pastirma* has become a popular sandwich filling in the United States, but the American type is tastier than the Turkish, and looks rather dif-

A Turkish drink seller.

ferent. The American type is also much more expensive.

Rather surprisingly, country people rarely take advantage of the fish which are plentiful in some of their many lakes and rivers. However, sea-fish are a popular food, although the fishing industry has not grown as quickly as the population figures.

In both town and country, the usual drinks are water, tea, and *ayran*. To make *ayran*, you simply add water to a few spoonfuls of yogurt, stir it, and perhaps add a little salt. Though wine is made in Turkey, and sold fairly cheaply, it is never drunk by Muslims who obey the rules of their religion. The Koran forbids drinking wine.

Many Turks drink no coffee, either, but the reason for that is different. Coffee is now too expensive for use in most households. However, the Turks are a very hospitable people and, as coffee is their traditional drink, they usually have some on hand to offer visitors. If it is prepared in the traditional way, it is served in small cups, black and very strong, and with so much sugar that it tastes rather like coffee-flavored treacle. With it, the guest may be offered some of the many sweets for which Turkey is famous. Turkish Delight really was invented in Turkey.

The Turks are very fond of sweets and sweet foods, so it is lucky for them that their country produces enough sugar (mainly from sugar beet) and honey for their needs. If it did not, they might well have to do without sweets as they have learned to do without coffee.

They have learned to do without coffee because coffee cannot be grown successfully in Turkey. The traditional Turkish coffee was grown in Arabia, and imported very cheaply when Arabia was part of the Ottoman Empire. But modern Arabia is independent of the Turkish Republic, and an important aim of the republic has been a self-sufficient Turkey—a Turkey using as far as possible only what Turkey herself can produce. It can produce tea, very good tea. And so the government charges such a high import duty on coffee that the Turks have become a nation of tea drinkers.

There are equally high duties on most other foreign goods. This has not only caused the Turks to use local goods instead, it has also caused some foreign firms to make their own goods in Turkey, employing Turkish workers and materials.

Turkey's governing body is still the Grand National Assembly, founded by Kemal Atatürk. The Grand National Assembly has an upper house, the Senate, and a lower house, the National Assembly. Members of both houses elect the president, and they themselves are elected by the people. The Senate also has 15 special members whom the president appoints.

Candidates from several parties contest the elections, but this has not always been so. Until Kemal Atatürk died (in 1938) and for some years afterward, Atatürk's Republican Party was the only party. There were also periods of military government in 1960 and 1961, and from September 1980 to November 1983. These followed some very severe economic troubles which the elected government could not settle. The present Grand National Assembly was democratically elected, and most Turks hope for regular elections in the future.

5

Up on the Plateau

On the Anatolian plateau, all roads lead to Ankara—as indeed do all railways and air routes. A visitor can hardly come up the 2,950 feet (900 meters) from sea level to plateau level without at least a glimpse of the capital city.

The glimpse will show a city which is almost wholly modern, spreading out from a rocky hill enclosed by the enormous turreted walls of an ancient fortress. And if he stops for more

Sitting on a wall above Ankara, a Turkish family admires the view.

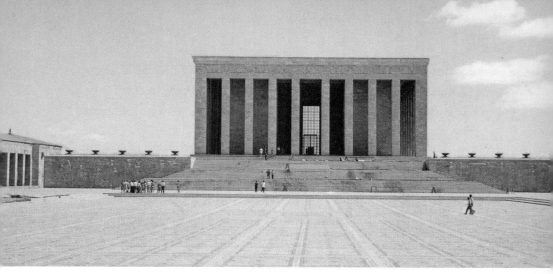

Kemal Atatürk's tomb.

than a glimpse, he will find himself in a well-planned city suffering from a serious growth problem—a city whose population has expanded from 30,000 to nearly three million in a little more than 70 years.

When Kemal Atatürk chose Ankara as the capital of the new Turkish Republic, neither he nor the town planners imagined that it would become so big. They designed and built a small, spacious, comfortable city with the government buildings in the center. The city was ringed by trees to soften the hard grey arid hills in the background. The new Ankara was, in fact, a garden city, and it remained a garden city as late as 1953, when Kemal Atatürk's body was moved to a huge new tomb in a hilltop memorial park at the edge of the built-up area.

Now, the tomb is well inside the built-up area. Ankara has

69

spread far beyond it, and out in all other directions. Many of the small buildings of the original garden city plan have been pulled down to make way for larger blocks in concrete and glass. By contrast, many of the new buildings on the outskirts of the city are the "up-in-a-night" shacks built by people who can find no other accommodation at a price they can afford, and who will not leave Ankara because their only prospect of work lies there.

However, all this human expansion has not squeezed out the storks who are old-established residents of Ankara—especially

The center of Ankara.

Storks—old-established residents of the Turkish capital.

of the ancient city within and near the fortress walls. Turks believe that good luck comes to a place where storks nest, and Ankara now has so many that it must feel very confident about its future.

The three million human residents are still mainly government workers and their families, but Ankara has become a city of light manufacturing industries, too, and it remains the chief marketing center for mohair (Angora wool) which comes from the long-haired goats bred in this part of Anatolia, and often seen on the hills beyond the city.

With several universities, its own symphony orchestra, opera and ballet, and a magnificent Museum of the Anatolian Civilizations, Ankara is also a leading educational and cultural center. However, it is mainly as a transportation center that Ankara appeals to most visitors. There is no other really comfortable and convenient base for exploring the rest of the plateau.

Nearly all such visitors think first of a look at the Göreme Valley, about 200 miles (320 kilometers) southeast of Ankara,

71

Mount Erciyas.

near the much smaller city of Kayseri. In early Christian times, Kayseri was the Roman city of Caesarea, capital of the imperial province of Cappadocia. Now it is best-known for its fine Seljuk buildings, its "mass-produced" *pastirma,* and its views of the old volcano, Mount Erciyas, which rises over 12,800 feet (3,900 meters) on the southern horizon. It used to be said that a climber on top of Mount Erciyas could see the Black Sea to the north and the Mediterranean to the south—more than 150 miles (240 kilometers) in each direction but nobody seems to have done so in modern times.

Over 10,000 years ago, when Mount Erciyas was still an active volcano, its eruptions covered this part of the plateau with a very thick layer of rock called tufa. Tufa is a soft rock, so soft that it is easily worn and shaped by the action of water and wind, and in the area west of Mount Erciyas, it has been worn into some very strange shapes indeed.

The area is a wide one, and much of it makes very rough

72

going for visitors, but luckily the most interesting part is also the easiest to reach and explore. This is the Göreme Valley, where the shapes are mainly pinnacles—tall, pointed columns of rock as much as 100 feet (30 meters) high, and massed in rows like a company of ghostly soldiers. In fact, an old Turkish story says that they really are just that—an invading army turned to stone in answer to the prayers of some poor peasants whom they were about to attack.

If the early Anatolian Christians knew that story, it does not seem to have worried them. When they were persecuted by the Romans, or harried in later invasions, many came to Göreme and settled in the valley as hermits, digging rooms for themselves in the soft rock of the pinnacles, and growing what food they needed in the rich volcanic soil. As time went on, many of the pinnacles became four- and five-storied houses honeycombed with the cells of hermits. Others were hollowed out to make chapels and churches, often beautifully decorated with painted patterns and pictures that can still be seen.

There are no hermits at Göreme nowadays, but people still live in the tufa. Here and in other parts of the district, farming

Houses in the tufa pinnacles.

people have hollowed out their homes in the sides of the valley, sometimes adding more conventional housefronts of cut stone.

Eastward of Mount Erciyas, Anatolia spreads across the upper reaches of the Euphrates and Tigris rivers, to Lake Van and the mountains of the eastern borders. Lake Van, 1,453 square miles (3,763 square kilometers) in area, stands 5,570 feet (1,700 meters) above sea level, but is much saltier than the sea, and can be just as stormy. Besides salt, its water contains a great deal of sodium carbonate, the "soda" that is used for washing clothes. If you are boating on the lake and hang your washing over the side, it will get clean as you go along, without any rubbing. Much of the salt and soda used throughout Turkey comes from Lake Van. Both substances are taken from the water by evaporation. Even more salt is taken from Lake Tuz, which lies in the driest part of the plateau, between Ankara and Konya, the old capital city of the Seljuk sultans. This area is so dry that Lake Tuz should really be called a salt-marsh rather than a lake, but the farmers of the area manage to grow good crops of grain and fruit in irrigated fields.

The wide uplands around Lake Van are one of the few parts of Turkey where you may hear large numbers of people speaking a native language that is not Turkish. These are the Kurds, a partly-nomad people who came here long before the original Turks, and who are also found over the borders in Iran, Iraq, and Syria. The Kurds regard this border country as their own, and many would like to occupy it as an independent nation.

74

However, neither Turkey nor any of its three neighbors has been willing to let it go, and Turkey seems to be even less willing since it has been developing the oilfields, coal seams, and other valuable mineral deposits that lie to the south and west of Lake Van. There has been an on-going violent revolution by the Kurds since 1983 to gain independence. The Turkish government has fought the uprising and the conflict continues to be waged.

Comprising 15 percent of Turkey's population, some Kurds have given up their old way of life and moved west, to work in industry, or even as dockers on the waterfront of Istanbul. However, most are still herdsmen and farmers, living in camps and villages spread over the southeastern uplands and as far north as the city of Erzurum, near the source of the Euphrates

Erzurum, in the extreme east of Turkey. It is Turkey's coldest and highest city.

Kurds in the Lake Van region.

(or Firat) River. At a height of 6,300 feet (1,920 meters) above sea level, Erzurum is the highest city in Turkey, and also the coldest.

Throughout the long, bitterly cold winter, icy winds and heavy snowstorms sweep across it, while the temperature stays permanently below freezing point. Nevertheless, nobody could think seriously of choosing a more comfortable site for the city. Not only is its present position the center of a very fertile farming area with great prospects for improvement. It is also a vital base for the defense of Anatolia. A glance at the map will show you why.

Erzurum has become a university center, too. Named after Kemal Atatürk, whose idea it was, the university has a special interest in farming. It runs a 10,000-acre (4,050-hectare) experimental farm to help the farmers and herdsmen of eastern Turkey improve their crops and their animals.

Apart from its university and its military installations, Erzurum is very much a farming town. Its industries—mainly leather tanning and the production of sugar from beet—are all connected with farming, and its trade is all in farm produce.

Much the same can be said of most other cities and major towns on the Anatolian plateau. If they have any manufacturing industries, these are mainly traditional craft industries—carpet-weaving, copper-beating, tile and pottery making. Even in Eskişehir, a city of 413,000 people west of Ankara, and the one big industrial center on the plateau, a traditional craft ranks high among the more modern industries. This is the making of tobacco pipes and ornaments from a lightweight local stone called by the German name *meerschaum*, which means sea-froth. In recent years Eskişehir has evolved into one of the largest industrial centers of Turkey, including industries in textiles, chemicals, railway and agricultural equipment.

New roads and railways, hydroelectricity, more farmland, and free education have certainly helped the people of the plateau to enjoy more comfortable lives and perhaps better prospects, and the plateau is still a source of food and raw materials for the rest of Turkey.

6

Around the Coasts

In Turkey's wish for self-sufficiency, there can be few more important places than a new seaport built at one of the most ancient human settlements in the world. This is Mersin, near the eastern end of the south coast of Anatolia, and about 17 miles (27 kilometers) from Tarsus, the birthplace of St. Paul. Mersin has been continuously settled for at least 8,000 years, but its importance to modern Turkey did not begin until 1962. Then, it became an oil-refining center and, through a huge manmade harbor, the outlet for Turkey's own oilfields. East of Mersin, and not far from Antakya (Antioch of the New Testament) oil reaches the Gulf of Iskenderun through a pipeline from the fields southwest of Lake Van, one of which has the rather surprising name of Batman.

Between Mersin and the Gulf of Iskenderun, three rivers come down to the sea through the fertile Plain of Çukurova, and one of these has been dammed to make an artificial lake about 10 miles (16 kilometers) north of Adana, Turkey's fourth-largest city. The dam not only provides Adana's industries with hydroelectric power. It also irrigates the Çukurova Plain, and so allows the farmers of the plain to harvest over 98,400 tons (100,000 tonnes) of cotton each year. Much of this is spun into thread and woven into cloth in the textile factories which employ many of Adana's 600,000 people.

Harvesting cotton is a slow and tiring job tor which the farmers need large numbers of helpers, and so harvest-time brings thousands of pickers from the plateau and the mountains down to the coast for a change of climate and better-paid work than they can find at home. Some of these are Yörüks—camel-riding nomads who, unlike the Kurds, are of the same race as the original Turks, and who speak an old dialect of the Turkish language. In their camps they weave very fine carpets, but only for themselves. They will not sell them to other people.

West of Adana and Mersin, much of the southern coast was more developed and more prosperous in Greek and Roman times than it is now. Every turn of the road seems to reveal the ruin of another ancient town or building, and some of them are not so ruinous. For instance, at Aspendos—about halfway between an ancient pirates' lair and the birthplace of Saint Nicholas—there is a huge Roman theater 1,800 years old but almost "as good as new." It can seat 20,000 people, and is still used for an annual drama festival and regular Turkish wrestling contests.

However, the 20th century is obvious, too. Not far inland, a waterfall has been harnessed to provide hydroelectricity for an aluminum smelting works, while the irrigated plain of Antalya is another cotton-producing area. Further inland, farmers in the lake district of Isparta make an important contribution to the French cosmetic industry by growing roses. From these, they distill oils which are exported to France and used as the base for many of the best-known French perfumes.

On the western coast lands, facing the Aegean Sea, the remains of ancient cities and civilizations stand out even more than they do in the south. This was the area of Troy, of Sardis the city of King Croesus, and of the great Greek city-states

A view of Izmir, Turkey's third largest city and her second largest port.

which contributed as much as Greece itself towards the shaping of European civilization.

Most of these city-states are now empty ruins, or at best small modern towns set among the ruins, but one of them, Izmir, has survived 3,000 years of fighting, fire, and earthquake to become the third largest city and the second seaport of modern Turkey. It is also a naval base and the site of Turkey's annual international fair, as well as the southeastern headquarters of the North Atlantic Treaty Organization (NATO), of which Turkey is a member.

Called Smyrna by the Greeks, Izmir kept its Greek name and a mainly Greek population until the end of the First World War (1918), when the Greeks of Europe tried to take this part of Anatolia. They were driven out by Kemal Atatürk's republican army, and most of Izmir's Greek residents went with them. However, the Turks of Izmir are just as proud as the Greeks before them to claim that their city was the birthplace of the Greek poet Homer, who wrote about the siege of Troy.

During the fighting at the end of the First World War, nearly three-quarters of Izmir—then mainly a wooden city—was destroyed by fire, and what remained was wrecked in an earthquake in 1928. Izmir is therefore a very modern city and, like Ankara, one that is not without its "up-in-a-night" shacks.

Until 1922, Izmir was known to the Turks as "Infidel Izmir," because the majority of its people were Christians. That was most unusual for modern Turkey, but in earlier times the whole of western Anatolia was a Christian area. As is shown by

81

The house of the Virgin Mary on Mount Ala, near Ephesus.

the books of the New Testament, many of its cities were among the first places visited by St. Paul and some other apostles, and St. John the Evangelist may have written his gospel at Ephesus, whose ruins lie to the south of Izmir, not far from the winding Menderes River. At that time, the river was known by the Greek names *Maiandros* or *Meander*, and that is why we now use the word "meander" for a long, looping bend in any river.

Ephesus—or Selçuk as the modern town is called—keeps up the ancient connection with Christianity. On a mountain to the south of the town, there is an ancient house where the Virgin Mary is said to have spent her old age, and every summer thousands of people set out from Selçuk on a pilgrimage to it. The house is now a Christian chapel, but many of the pilgrims are Muslims—Muslims believe that Jesus was a great prophet, and so they revere his mother.

The west coast ends on the windy plain of Troy, where some of the ancient Trojan city (but *not* the wooden horse) has been excavated from a great mound called Hissarlik. Then, beyond

82

the southern shores of the Sea of Marmara and a mountain called Uludağ, the Black Sea coast begins.

Over 8,300 feet (2,540 meters) high, Uludağ is a winter sports resort for the people of Istanbul, and a camping ground for the nomad herdsmen called Yörüks. Below it to the north lies the city of Bursa, the original Ottoman capital and the burial place of some of the Ottoman sultans.

A visitor who has been on the snow slopes above Bursa will hardly want to swim in the Sea of Marmara, but he may well enjoy the naturally hot spring water in one of Bursa's several *hamams*, or Turkish baths. Like Turkish delight, the Turkish bath really *was* invented in Turkey, and no town is without at least one public *hamam.*

Bursa is also an ancient center of the silk-growing, silk-weaving, and knife-making industries, and—a more modern development—of such sheet-metal industries as car-body making. The sheet metal comes from steel mills close to the coalfields around Zonguldak, a small port on the Black Sea coast.

The Pontic Mountains along the Black Sea coast are rich in several useful minerals, though the gold and silver for which the area was once famous are now played out. As far as the gold is concerned, perhaps that is not surprising. From the old Greek story of Jason and the Golden Fleece, we know that people were already taking gold from here about 3,500 years ago.

The place where Jason obtained the Golden Fleece is outside Turkey, in the neighboring Russia. But the people from whom he obtained it were perhaps the ancestors of a non-Turkish

83

community called Laz, who live in the coastal valleys at the eastern end of Black Sea Turkey. The Laz are much less numerous than the Kurds, probably numbering no more than about 30,000, but they cling to their own Indo-European language.

These eastern Black Sea coast lands are the wettest part of Turkey. With a rainfall of around 100 inches (254 centimeters) a year, and very fertile soil, they could almost be called cool jungle country. This makes them ideal for growing tea, and the whole of Turkey's large tea crop is grown here, as well as rice, nuts, and a great deal of fruit. Some of the farmers also produce honey—from hives fixed high in trees to keep bears away.

As on the Aegean coast, most of Turkey's Black Sea towns began life as ancient Greek settlements, but none was ever as big or as important as the Aegean city-states, and the one which became famous did so much later. This was Trapezos, now called Trabzon, which managed to survive as an independent Byzantine Christian kingdom for nearly 400 years after the Turks came to Anatolia.

Trabzon's smaller neighbor Giresun also deserves to be

The porch of the church of St. Sophia, Trabzon.

Locally grown fruit in a Turkish market.

famous, but it is difficult to see that the name hides a Greek name from which comes our word "cherry." The first cherry trees ever grown in Europe were brought there from Giresun, in the first century A.D.

Trabzon and Giresun are both marketing and shipping centers for the farm products of the coast lands and mountain slopes behind them—mainly nuts, tobacco, and fruit. So too are most other Black Sea towns, apart from the coal and steel centers of Zonguldak and Ereǧli. West of Zonguldak, there are only seaside resorts, mainly for vacationers from Ankara and they lead us into Europe, to Trakya (Thrace) and Istanbul.

7

Turkey in Europe

Trakya is the Turkish name for Turkey's foothold in Europe, the corner of ancient Thrace which was the first part of Europe to be conquered by the Ottoman sultans, and the only part which they were still holding when Turkey became a republic.

Its heart, of course, is the great city of Istanbul, and so much is heard of this heart that people are sometimes inclined to forget the body around it—9,300 square miles (24,000 square kilometers) of farmland, hill pasture, and forestry plantation, and another city which, like Istanbul, was once the capital.

The other city is Edirne, 146 miles (235 kilometers) northwest of Istanbul, near the borders separating Trakya from Greece and Bulgaria. This position puts Edirne astride the main route from central Europe into Trakya, and explains why the Ottoman sultans used it as their capital while Istanbul was still holding out against them.

They made good use of their time in Edirne. No other city of its size contains so many fine buildings in the old Turkish

Preparing for oiled wrestling championships, Edirne.

style. The four minarets of its main building, the great Selimiye mosque, make a landmark that can be seen from far away, and show travelers from the west that they have entered a Muslim country. There is also a building of a kind now fairly rare in Turkey—a Jewish synagogue. Edirne, like Istanbul, has had a Jewish community since the Middle Ages.

Apart from its buildings, Edirne has one other attraction for visitors—a national festival of Turkish wrestling, held every summer on an island in the Tunca River.

The road from Edirne to Istanbul runs straight across a dry plain where the farmers grow grain, tobacco, and sunflowers. They grow the sunflowers not for the flowers themselves, but

87

for the seeds. These give an oil which is used in making margarine, and can be used in cooking as a substitute for the more expensive olive oil of which Turks are very fond. The seed crops are exported from Tekirdağ, a small seaport in a grape-growing district on the shore of the Sea of Marmara.

South and west of Tekirdağ, Trakya becomes hilly, with small ranges rising to about 3,000 feet (915 meters). Beyond these hills, at the entrance to the Sea of Marmara, lies the Gallipoli Peninsula, where British, Australian, and New Zealand troops landed early in the First World War. Their object was to block the Dardanelles (the straits leading into the Sea of Marmara) and then capture Istanbul, but a Turkish force led by Kemal Atatürk drove them back.

The Dardanelles, once called the Hellespont by the Greeks and now called the Straits of Cannakkale by the Turks, are about 45 miles (72 kilometers) long and, at their narrowest, about one mile (1.6 kilometers) wide. It was at this narrowest width that the Persians built a bridge of boats for their attack on Greece in 480 B.C., and the British poet Byron swam the straits in 1810 A.D. Byron's object was to match the feats of Leander, who in an old Greek story swam the straits regularly. Visitors find that rather confusing when they go to Istanbul at the other end of the Sea of Marmara. There, they are told that Leander did his swimming in the Bosporus, nearly 200 miles (320 kilometers) from the point where Byron crossed. However, it is the people of Istanbul who are wrong. The Dardanelles are the real straits of the story.

Running northwest from the Bosporus, roughly parallel with the Edirne-Istanbul road, are the Istranca Mountains. The southern slopes of these mountains are dry and fairly bare, in many places fit only for grazing goats, but the northern slopes, facing the Black Sea, are very well watered. Here, there were ancient forests which were gradually cut down for building timber and fuel during Ottoman times. They have now been replaced by new and carefully managed conifer plantations. In some plantations, there are picnic sites and playgrounds much used by the people of Istanbul.

It is this forest area that gives Istanbul most of its water supply. The water reaches the city from a system of reservoirs and aqueducts begun by the Byzantines, improved by the Ottomans, and brought up to date in modern times to try to

The one-time church of St. Sophia, Istanbul—one of the finest examples of Byzantine art.

meet the needs of the 12 million people who now live in Istanbul.

If a visitor is more interested in variety of people than in variety of places, and has little time for travel, he will not be disappointed if he stays in Istanbul. Istanbul's population doubled in the 20 years between 1955 and 1975, and has grown by over half a million a year since then. Most of the increase came not from births but from immigration. So the chances are strong that every third person a visitor meets will have come from some other part of Turkey. There is no corner of the country, and no racial type found anywhere in the country—not even Kurds, Yörüks, and Laz—unrepresented among the workers of modern Istanbul.

Most of these immigrants came to the city looking for work in the fast-developing factory industries, and many of them live on the Asian side of the Bosporus, in a spreading industrial area that begins with the old suburb of Üsküdar.

Üsküdar is perhaps better known as Scutari, a fact which sometimes surprises visitors who are interested in Florence Nightingale and her army nursing service. Because she began the service during the Crimean War (1853-1856), it is often imagined that her famous "Lady with the lamp" hospital was actually at Crimea, on the northern shore of the Black Sea. However, it was in fact at Üsküdar, facing old Istanbul across the Bosporus, and Istanbul built a training school for nurses in memory of her.

When they were well enough to look at it, her patients would have seen what many people still think is the most beautiful city skyline in the world—the mosques, churches, palaces and towers of old Istanbul, spread over seven hills on a peninsula made by the Bosporus, the Sea of Marmara and the Golden Horn, and backed by a huge defensive wall about four miles (six and a half kilometers) long, 13 feet (four meters) thick, and in parts 65 feet (20 meters) high.

Built by the Byzantine emperors, this wall once continued for eight miles (13 kilometers) around the three-sided waterfront, and was the main reason why the city held out against the Ottomans for more than a century. At that time, the defenses were completed by a chain barrier across the mouth of the Golden Horn, Istanbul's natural harbor.

The Golden Horn has its name because, when seen from a height on a sunny day, it looks rather like a gilded goat horn— a goat horn about four miles (six and a half kilometers) long. It is now crossed by three bridges, the newest and furthest inland being a highway bridge, built so that vehicles can bypass the old city on their way to the Bosporus Bridge. Next, linking some new streets and shopping developments in the old city with the suburbs to the north of the Golden Horn, is the Ataturk Bridge. And then, right at the mouth of the Golden Horn, is the older and very well-known Galata Bridge.

The Galata Bridge, whose central section opens once a day to let shipping through, is as much a pleasure promenade as a practical roadway between old Istanbul and its northern sub-urb Galata. As it floats on iron pontoons, the pontoons are a lower "story" where it is possible to have a meal, do some shopping, listen to gypsy music, try to catch fish, have your shoes cleaned, or just stroll around watching the people and admiring the views.

Galata, at the northern end of the bridge, was originally independent of Istanbul. Merchants from Italy, mainly Genoese, founded it as a self-governing trading settlement, and they left a memorial to themselves in the form of the tall Galata Tower. This tower commands a view over the whole Istanbul area, and was used by watchmen looking for the approach of invaders, or the first signs of fire when most of Istanbul's houses were made of wood. Visitors can now enjoy the panorama as they take a Turkish meal in a restaurant at the top.

Beyond Galata, newer suburbs now stretch far up the Bosporus, overlooking the enormous 365-room white marble palace of Dolmabahçe, built in 1853 by a sultan who wanted a home more modern and more western in style than Topkapi, the ancient and very oriental-looking palace of the sultans in old Istanbul.

Like the famous Saint Sophia church which stands fairly near it, Topkapi is now a museum, while Dolmabahçe is used for special occasions by the Turkish government, and sometimes as a residence for the president or his guests. Kemal Atatürk was in residence here when he died in 1938.

If he was there now, he could look north and see, a short distance up the Bosporus, the latest step in his plan for bringing Turkey into the modern world—the handsome span of the

Topkapi Palace, Istanbul, now a museum.

Bosporus Bridge which makes his country more than ever the link in culture and commerce between its neighbors in the east and its neighbors in the west.

8

Turkey in the World

There is more to Turkey's place in the modern world than its role as a bridge between the peoples and civilizations of Asia and Europe. After the Second World War, it had the delicate and difficult task of keeping up its traditional interests and friendships in the west, while improving relations with its traditional enemy and most powerful neighbor, the Soviet Union.

It managed to balance its connections with the two sides very well, and both gave practical help with its plans for industrial development and self-sufficiency. Help from the former Soviet Union included the building of several hydroelectricity plants. From the United States and Britain, Turkey received about five million U.S. dollars and 100 million British pounds towards the cost of developing its factory industries and improving its agriculture.

In addition, as Turkey's long coastline and land boundaries made it necessary for it to spend more money than it can afford on its armed services, the United States helped it to meet the cost. This is because Turkey is a member of the North Atlantic

Treaty Organization (NATO), and therefore committed to a part in western defense.

As a country on two continents, Turkey made its position clear by joining the European Community as an associate member, and the Central Treaty Organization (CENTO), which linked it with the Asian countries, Iran, and Pakistan. Turkey has recently applied for full membership in the European Union (EU). The international highway from the Bosporus Bridge through Turkey and Iran to the Indian subcontinent was partly a CENTO project.

In western Europe, associate membership of the European Community not only opened markets for Turkey's exports. It also provided opportunities for over 500,000 Turks to find well-paid work in the more prosperous European Community countries. This has done much more for Turkey than easing its unemployment problem. Nearly all the migrant workers send some of their wages home, or take their savings home after two or three years, and the money has done much to narrow an unfavorable gap in Turkey's balance of payments.

However, Turkey has two neighbors with whom its relations have not been so happy. One of these is Greece, and the other is Cyprus—the large Mediterranean island less than 50 miles (80 kilometers) from the south coast of Anatolia.

Cyprus was part of the Ottoman Empire until 1878, but was then taken over by Britain, and has since become an independent republic. Its population is partly Greek, partly Turkish, with Greeks making the majority, and the two peoples have

95

not been able to live and govern themselves as a national partnership. Some Greek Cypriots would prefer the island to become part of Greece, and they tried to achieve their aim by armed rebellion in 1974. They were given support by the Greek government of the time, which was subsequently overthrown, and this support led to a civil war in which Turkey invaded Cyprus to help and protect the Turkish Cypriots. The fighting did not last long but Turkey has kept its troops on the island and, in 1983, the Turkish Cypriots declared their part of Cyprus to be an independent republic. The new republic has not been recognized by the United Nations Organization. In fact, Turkey is the only member nation who does recognize it. The Cyprus problem is one of the reasons sighted for Turkey not yet being granted full membership in the European Union.

Turkey fully supports the United Nations Organization (UN), of which it was an early member, and (in the Korean War of 1950) one of the first members to provide troops for a United Nations purpose. Since then, it has continued to take an active and useful part in making the work of the United Nations effective, especially in its policies of improving the conditions and prospects of "Third World" countries.

The Kurdish rebellion in the south continues to plague Turkey. The conflict there has been a violent one leading to world accusations of human rights violations by the Turks. Turkey's problems with the Greeks in Cyprus and the Kurds within their own country are holding the country back from a respected place in the international community.

Turkey faces economic problems, with inflation at more than 90 percent in 1998. Its cities are bursting at the seams and there are overcrowding and infrastructure problems.

Turkey goes into the 21st century still trying to balance its allegiance between the East and the West, and trying to keep its own traditions and values in the process.

GLOSSARY

Anatolia   The Asian part of Turkey

ayran   A drink made by adding water to yogurt with a little salt

fez   A stiff red hat usually worn by Turkish men prior to the reforms of 1923

hamams   Turkish baths, in which a person passes through a series of steam rooms that grow increasingly hotter, followed by a massage and cold shower

Janissaries   A regiment of highly-trained soldiers who served the Ottoman Empire as the sultan's guards and troops

Koran   The holy book of the Muslim religion

Kurds   A nomadic people who have lived in parts of Turkey, Syria, Iran, and Iraq since very early times. They are in a war with Turkey for their independence.

minarets   The tall thin towers on mosques from which a time for prayer is called

mohair	A very soft wool made from the hair of Angora goats bred in Turkey and other coutries in the area
mosque	Temple of the Islam religion
nomads	Tent-dwelling herders who move from place to place seeking grazing land for their flocks
Slejuks	A group of Turks who invaded the area called Anatolia in 1037. They became the first Turks in the area that would eventually become Turkey.
Turkish delight	A jellylike sweet candy cut in cubes and dusted with sugar
Yörüks	Nomads of Turkish descent

INDEX